HELLO, SUNLIGHT

Eastyn Star

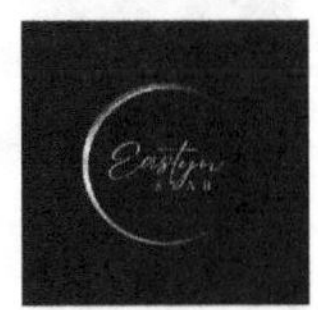

*This book is dedicated to the love of my life - thank you for sticking with me throughout it all. These poems are a reflection of a love so true, and that's worth every single bit of love that I have inside of me to give to you daily. This book is dedicated to the lovers who no matter how hard
it gets, you still find a way to stay. This is dedicated to those who still believes in love, just know that there is someone out there for you.*

To my children - keep climbing high, I see y'all. I love you!

I chose to run through the fields while the grass was burning,
Forging forward with the intent to gain the experiences of the wild.
Where others chose to take the safest route for survival,
I needed to conquest this path just to earn the badge of being a warrior.

- EASTYN STAR

CONTENTS

HELLO, SUNLIGHT

Strolling through the garden
of calamitous, Where the
rabid animals run ravenous.
Trusting the wrong person will
be your doom, Smiling in your
face while being led into a fantasy
room.
Just to devour you & you're not
missed, You no longer exist,
Taking the wrong path where it's
long & twisted.

If you make it out alive, you will never be the
same, Treacherous game play led to you no
longer remembering your name.
Pleading to be taken away,
You don't want to feel anymore pain.

Then eventually, it starts to make
sense, You start living in the
present,

Building your strength to be in the
moment, You felt paralyzed,
Now you can feel some movement.
The sun shines bright,
Smiling, you say, "Hello, Sunlight."

ENTICING AFFAIR

Sequential patterns form a
rhythm to the beat, Invoking
your body to speak-
Speak to me in ways to let me know
that you're yearning.
I need to hear the depths of every
sharp breath that you intake,
While I show you high octane levels
to ignite the fuel that you've chosen
to boldly innovate.

Let me feel your tongue move
in syllables pressing against my
inner thighs,
Conducting your own investigation on how
shall I reach my highest of heights.
Preparing yourself to swim
deep into a thunderstorm, A
thunderstorm prepared to rip you
into shreds with one stroke.

Somehow, perfectly learning me as your

student as you further instruct this
course,
Astonishing me with each
breaststroke through this surge,
Igniting the pilot and utilizing the
control panel to combust the fumes
into a fire,
Setting off the sprinkler to cool
down the blazing inferno,
Still, with persistence, you pull the
turbo.

In your most elevated teaching, we reach
our last systematic lesson,
Ruling out teaching is your best
profession.
Lying still in a pool full of liquids oozing
from the gentle sides of us,
**Slumbering deeply with nothing but
love.**

PURE LOVE

Pure love,
Pure intimacy,
Pure ecstasy,
Gliding through the times of devotion.
Just tell me it's all mine.
The reassurance is all I need, babe.

I never expected perfect, but you're perfect for me.

You waited for me. You grew with
me.
Strength beyond the industrial
revolution we've built,
Never want to let this go,
So I'm caught going with the flow,
The flow that led to extravagant
encounters, Also, moments filled
with smiles and laughter.

Date nights beyond my wildest
imagination,

Followed by alone time that I
couldn't ever imagine.
Complementing me in more ways
than one, how it's supposed to be,
In the bed, I become your own
personal freak.

Pure love,
Fully a dream come true.
All I want is for you to continue
loving me like you do,
Because I'm in love with you.

ACQUIRED TASTE

When it flows like the
highest key of the piano,

There, it whispers softly more words
than you could ever imagine.
Together lies the winding turns of our
mistakes,
But I'm so engulfed with the love you
bring to me,
The joy you bring to my life is my
favorite acquired taste.

Manifested the love that we have,
I am so grateful for who you've become.

We've had a long trip around the sun 365
days 20 times,
I've watched the changes you've made
over the years.

Grown from a boy into a man,
The highs & the lows of where it all
began -
We had no clue what we were getting
ourselves into,

We were just kids.
We grew apart just for us to mold
together,
Just promise me forever -

When it flows effortlessly without having to force it

CITY LIGHTS

Pristine view of the Las Vegas' city lights,

Mesmerized by the look in your
eyes,
As we view the strip from the
balcony on the 50th floor,
Fully knowing what this night has
in store.

Captivated by the days that we spent
for my birthday, Exposing your
romantic side in increments,
Leaving little room for me to say -
I'm completely speechless.

Slow motion strokes while the rest
of the world parties,
Excitement fills the space of the
balcony,
Immersed in our current fantasy.

Kissing me slowly to break away
from our allure,
Looking forward to what else you
have planned - mi amor.

Hearing the water from the whirlpool
tub,
Smiling - Oh, how madly I'm in love.
Never have I ever had anyone who
made me feel so special,
& never have I ever had anyone be so
gentle.

Living in the stages of pure bliss,
Not wanting to end from a time like
this.
If time could stand still - would be
my only wish.

In a world of woe,
Secrets remain that we will never
tell a soul,
**As we are consumed by the city
lights.**

NOVA

I'm grateful for you.
Everything that we do is always
brand new.
We had to go our separate ways, Just
for us to be where we are today.

They said that real love never dies,
Even when I wanted to let go,
Here we are again in rotation
clockwise.
Starting to feel like this is meant to
be,
My soulmate - I am confident that
God made you for me.

We're a nova in the sky.
A new star - that burns so bright,
That everyone across the globe can see us.

When we slowly dim,
We find a way to keep the same

intensity.
Achieving heights and depths that
show our luminosity.
Paving a path for all to show off
our generosity,
Proving that even on the darkest
days,
**Not even force can deter us from
our destiny.**

PERFECT VIEW

Perfect view
With the shades drawn,
So the world will know what we
plan to do.
Just us two.

Waiting for a planned visit,
Adding a third to expose a side of
us that shows no limits,
Exposing a side of us where we can
indulge,
Concentrating on the flavors
that appear within the sky like a
rainbow.

Developing a high that has no down,
Exploring a new life for us now,

As this mystery woman appears,
I let go of my fears.

As I kiss her slowly,
I allow my desires to take full

control over me.
Gripping her breast as I hear the
softest moan,
I look over to see him hard as a
stone.

Licking my lips,
**I prepare myself to sail the harbor
on our love nest ship.**

PRESSURE BURSTS PIPES

I never saw you as ordinary,
You've always been
extraordinary.
The purity of your heart and mind,
Even when you're at your lowest,
You never switched up - you stayed
kind.

You're hard on yourself because you
see your potential,
So I'm writing this letter to you as a
reminder that you're special.

Your smile brightens up someone's
day,
& your laugh makes the next person
laugh with you like crazy.
So hold your head up while you

work on building yourself back up.

You're always so positive with
others around you,
But when it comes to yourself -
you're so pessimistic.
Always in your head and
wondering about what the future
may hold.
Baby, you don't know what is going
to hold, time to learn how to be
optimistic.

Stand in your truth, but learn how
to take it easy,
Have fun for once, you deserve it.

You put so much work in, loosen up
a bit.

Let go of your self-doubts and the
past pains and hurt,
Not everyone is out to get you, Or
trample you in the dirt.

You're a beautiful soul,
Elegant as they come.
No one is like you,
So why do you dim your light to allow
anyone to outshine you?
Why do you hold back and allow
what you've been through to keep you
victimized?
Why have you allowed life to take its

final toll?
Why do you feel the need to stay in
control?

You are only a victim to your
circumstances as long as you allow
yourself to be,
What was done, you can never go
back and change,
& what is before you is a whole
world full of opportunities and
happiness.

Heal so that you can live your life
in authenticity. Heal so that you
can pour more into yourself and
others,
Heal so that you can stop bleeding
on those trying to love you,
Heal so that you can stop allowing
your triggers to override your
intuition,
And believing that it is your
intuition,
Heal so that you can rebuild & stop
looking at yourself as the enemy.

Heal so that you can live in the
moment & understand your vision.
Heal so that you can stop hoping,
praying, and wishing,

Wishing for a better life when you
are the only one in your own way.
Searching for the moment to
escape,

Escape from a room that is filled with tricks
and mazes,
Clowns with pretty painted faces,
Leading you to a dark and deadly
dead end.

You are in total control of your
future,
Remember that you're a winner and
not a loser,
Stop being hard on yourself for your
mistakes,
Everyone goes through the highs
and lows,
Nothing worth having comes
unchallenging.
Also, remember to take a break.
A mental and physical break.

You work too hard for perfection,
But aren't so welcoming to
corrections.
Life's all about correction and then
redirection.
You got this,
If no one believes in you - just
know I do.
Be the pressure that you've aways
dreamed about.

Reminder to self: Pressure bursts pipes.

NOTE TO SELF, TIME
TO GO HARDER
FOR YOURSELF.

SEISMIC ZONE

Surf the waves that appear before
us with so much density.
Us together, we'll never drown.
For our love holds barrows filled
with the world's greatest form of
immensity.

We have survived substantial tests
time and time again,
Before we were lovers, we were
friends.
I'll treasure you until the end.

No one holds me down the way that
you do,
& no one could compare to this love
that has proven to be so true.
Two decades later, & all I see is you.

FOREPLAY

Recollecting on all of the time we spent.

Hold up, wait...

How about the times you pulled my dress up after another great date with pleasuring ourselves in the wide open? I'm going to need to run that back, Exercising the right to take it how far you want to go.

Undeniable desires blaze a fire tonight, Remember all the times that I used to drive you wild? Lying back chiefin' while I seduced you with my moves, Eyes glazed over in lust, While I moved your hand every time you tried to touch my bust.

I needed you to watch me in this

foreplay,
As I drive your body crazy.
I'm ready for a wild night,
Not a long time.
Give me all the things that you
know that I like.

Push me back on the bed,
Grab a handful of my hair,
Instructing me to watch you go to
work,
Looking at me with a smirk,
I love the cockiness.
Knowing that you have a reason to
show your arrogance.

Raise my temperatures to an
extreme,
Capsizing an arousal that leads to a
midstream.
Puddling all over the black satin
sheets,
Urging your lips to continuously
kiss the honeypot that's grown so
sweet.

Covering my mouth with a pillow to
soften each moan,
Pushing it away, telling me that
we're all alone.

Not a soul can hear us,
We're ravishing in these hidden sins
where we lay,
But this is only foreplay.

COLLIDE

Take me back to the night when
the full moon was high in the
sky,
While we watched the waves
collide,
As you kissed in between my inner
thighs.
We were at an all-time high.
We made love that night.

STIMULATION

I had thirsted for my soul to be fed
just as much as I had hungered
for the inclination of mental
stimulation.
Never known a love like this,
This love has me at the highest of heights, looking down at the
elevation.

I am not afraid of the fall, it's a
thrill to my soul.
Hoping that this lasts for a lifetime.
**An eternal flame that could never
be put out - it burns brighter as the
years goes by mi amor.**

BABY LOVE

His protectiveness
obscures from others to
see,
Until his fangs show,
He doesn't play about me.
He is as deadly as a knight's sword,
He is the king on the chessboard.
He shows his unwaved loyalty and
admiration,
So I hold him down as his queen to
his entire nation.

Whenever he's in despair,
I pick up the pieces to show him
that I am there.
If he needs someone to listen to,
No matter the hour,
I come through.

I am the foundation where he lays
his bricks,

Peaceful and a rare sight to see - we
are a lunar eclipse.
I motivate him to live out his
wildest endeavors,
With me by his side,
It's been a game-changer for the
better.

Monstrous to the world,
Yet, I accompany him to bring out
his softer side.
Providing a safe haven for him to
feel secure,
His cold heart thaws, unlocking the
gentlest intimate moments alive.
I am like pudding in his arms,
He holds an irresistible allure.

We, in unison like a mirror's
reflection, Undefeatable by nature,
Perfectly constructed into a
soulmate connection.
I gaze into his eyes to understand
him,
Grasping the concept of learning
so that I can fully embrace his
imperfections.

I feed him with submissions,
Allowing him to lead,
While I follow his direction.
I allow him to bring out my

feminine side in return. Fire
exchanges without warning is like
watching acres burn.

Engulfed and surrounded with
pleasantries that we could never
tell,
Multiple people have risen up
against us, but we never fell.
Forevermore in our castle will we
remain.
I provide peace when his
environment is chaotic,
   He knows that resting on my
   breast puts him in a hypnotic
   state of mind.

This love affair is symbolic,
Our locked-on stare without touching
is excitingly erotic.
Bringing out his happiness,
In exchange, I receive tenderness.
Unimaginable bond with seeds of love
and faithfulness.
**Gracefully, I can say that I am his
Baby Love.**

MAJESTIC

Let's make magic underneath the stars, Unbothered by the cold breeze against our skin.
We'll wrap our blanket around us
to feel our body heat,
Unconcerned about who catches
us.
Spontaneity at its finest,
We're like teenagers all over again.

WATERFALL

Let's escape to a waterfall full
of promises.
There, you can have me
where the rain pours and showers
you with my sweet love.
We don't need an umbrella - you
love how it coats you.

Hand and hand as we dance,
Spinning in circles until we both
tire ourselves from this great
escapade.
You love the wild child in me that I
let loose on this crusade,
Conquering inches deep inside my
honey pot
Adjusting and swallowing you like a
dangerous undercurrent.
Yet, you arise for the challenge.

You're so brave as I stare you in the
eyes,
Shadowing the walls as the figures

tells tall stories of these concurrent
events - that takes place when our
bodies tantalize,
Tantalizing and preparing the
ship that will cross the great blue
millions of times,
Dominating unexplored sunken
secrets beneath the Black Sea.

Behold a land full of undiscovered
treasuries,
Climbing Mt. Everest until we reach the
highest elevation,
Satisfaction and plummeting into a
comfortable silence,
**Scanning the motherland where we
shall build our empire.**

ENCHANTMENT

Speak to my soul as I breathe air into yours.
Together, we have the perfect balance of ways to ground our love. Multiplying opportunities that will soon hold the key to opening up the golden door.

One that leads us into the sunshine where the garden forever blooms with peonies and white lilies, Decorated with gnomes as frogs splash in the pond next to the red-hot chilies. Rounding about the area where we bask in the moments ahead, Vowing never to look back to how things were before.

Slowly understanding how to analyze the arch of destiny. Incredible experiences that

complete a simple rhythmical
melody.

Structure holding fast to uphold any blows
sent to defeat our empire,
Enacting the stages of healing through the
past that exerts us to reach higher.
**Throughout it all, we found a flow that
meshes well with our divine enchantment.**

LADY OF RADIANCE

Goddess vibes,
Magical mound between my thighs,
I'll lift you high when you feel the lowest.

Queen vibes,
The rarest of the rare, but my actions are more than words can be described.
No, I am not the easiest to understand,
& yes, there are times when I'm hard to comprehend .

So I lay out the blueprint.
Pay attention to my body language.
My body language is comparable to sign language.
It provides more words than I could ever manage.
Stay focused on me & I'll move more

than just mountains.

Wifey vibes,
I'm loyal to my soil.
I'll never stray away, even times
gets rough.
I'll fight for you when things get
too tough.
I'm the ear that listens when you're
having a bad day,
& I'll still hold your hand when
things aren't going your way.

But I need your full commitment &
loyalty for me to go hard for you,
**As much love I'll have, I'll never
play the fool.**

NOSE WIDE OPEN

I'll love you through all of your phases.
I'll still cherish you throughout the ages.

Bury your secrets without any trace.

Still find you within the hidden maze.

That's how deep my love runs for you.

ENDLESSLY YOURS

Laying skin to skin couldn't
make me feel close enough,
I still crave your touch.
Days apart, I miss you,
You wouldn't understand the
motions that I go through.
I get giddy like a teenager again
when I see you smile, Then my eyes
light up when I hear about your
dreams & aspirations,
I love the sparkle in your eyes when
you talk about it.

I still love seeing you smile.
In the bedroom, I enjoy that we
follow each other's lead with our
wildest imaginations.
I hate seeing you sad,
I always try to find ways to cheer
you up.
I got it for you real bad.
When I miss you, I act up and get
mad.

I love that you push me to be a
better me,
I enjoy seeing the person you've
grown to be.
Watched you grow from a boy to a
man,
I'm going to forever root for you -
I'm your biggest fan.

I love you more than these words that
I tried to express,
I cherish the moments that we spend,
if I can confidently confess,
**Confess that I'm going to forever
want this.**

LOVE STORY

There could be a billion and one suitors, but I'll always choose you,
We could be a million miles away, and I'll always come through.
No one has my heart - I'll always love you,
Forever is what I proposed, so you'll know that I'll always stay true.

Nobody gets me like you do,
No one understands my mood swings but you.
I have never met someone who is just as intuitive as I am,
You're not just my lover - you're my best friend.

When my mood is dark,
You find solutions to make me smile.
After all these years,

I still wonder how, when I'm in
your presence, I'm completely
beguiled.

When we're making love, we are
fully embodied into one,
Skin to skin,
Our emotions heightened as we
further ascended.
Ascend through the elements of
sheer closeness.

For what we treasure beyond
the naked eye has become so
immersive,
What's understood about us is
comprehensive,
**So I return the love tenfold in this
love story.**

PILLOW TALK

See, I hope that this would be a
time that you listen,

And I always hope that you could
feel me even when we're at a
distance.
Tap further into my energy and
telepathically give me kisses.

> Do you feel where it's painful?
> Are you able to stare me deep into
> the eyes even when my actions are
> the most shameful?
> Most times, it hurts when I'm away
> from you.

I've grown attached to the man
who hides his romantic side from
the world because you feel like they
don't deserve your vulnerability,
And I've fallen in love with your
humility.
The fact that you care as deeply as
you do about everyone involved

with you,
It awakens me like the freshness of
morning dew.

I enjoy it when your eyes glisten
while you talk about your passions,
I melt in your arms when you send
my body through wild sensations.

In my mind, I see us until the end
of time - glorifying the stages of
immortality.
Embarking towards our destiny.
Treading away from what used to
be,
With faith that this is truly meant
to be.

So I hope that you understand how
hard it is to leave you,
And I hope that your love for me
forever stays true. Because, to be
honest, **I can't envision what my
life would be like without us as
one**.

LOVE LANGUAGE

On a different plain,
Further than the 5th dimension,
Leaping through portals feeling like we took some shrooms.

The area before us is full of colors and different shapes,

Where we don't need any words.

Our bodies speak the language of the trees.
Engulfed in one another, we are laying in the high grass of the forest.
Butterflies flying nearby, and all we hear is nature.
The live oak shading us from the brightness of the sun.
Laughing and touching one another - I come undone.

Allowing my walls to come down and letting in vulnerability.
You're understanding of every second, so you provide the

tranquility.
It's unnerving to comprehend the
moments with you I feel the most
alive,
The way you balance my libra scale
in all aspects where we can both
thrive.

I get so caught up in this feeling
that I feel every time I'm not with
you - it may just be our undoing,
Your soothing words let me know
that I am the queen of this castle -
it's my world and my ruling.
There's nothing that I wouldn't do
for you, let me show you.
So let your wall down, and trust
me, my body language is your cue.

Allowing my love to keep speaking
my love language,
We can both let go of our heavy
baggage.
Vanquishing our hidden tangles,
Smoothening them out in every
crevice and all angles.
We begin parading like wild beasts
in the animal kingdom.
Take better care as we're lounging
in the lion's den - we are the pride,
and you're the king, so full of
wisdom.

Your touch sends my mound
pulsating like reggae music
blowing from the speakers.
I am surprised by my aggression as
I beckon for you to go deeper.
I love the words you speak into my
ear - lullabying me to sleep like
you're the crypt keeper.
Steal my soul away - this fruit is
only getting sweeter.
Devour me so that I can see what
you're made of. To be able to hear
the words that you speak out of
love - **I want to learn your love
language too.**

FOR KEEPS

Before I ever let go of control,
I need to know that you
aren't going to fold,
Fold under pressure when things
get too rough.
Stay with me when things get too
tough.

See, I've been having this guard
up for years
Due to plenty of men who have
come into my life & caused so many
tears.
I play defense because of my fears,
But I'm standing here letting you
know that I'm here.

I'm wise enough to know how the
story goes,
Yet I'm giving you a chance to see
me without any clothes.
I'm not talking about naked in that
aspect,

I'm talking about exposing my mind to
you.

Will I be still respected?

Show up for me to continuously
feed my mind with intellect?
I am a sexual woman, but I get
turned on by the mind,
I need to know that it's me that you
choose every time.
I'm a selfish woman. I want you to
myself,
Not in the business of sharing.

I'm like a wolf when it comes to
mine.
I'm really possessive. I understand
my flaws,
I'm only human.

Before you walk down this one-way
street,
I need to know that you're going to
take care of me, Physically,
Emotionally, Mentally,
And spiritually.
I want years, not months.
I'm playing for keeps.

GREENER PASTURES

G alloping into the open field
like a stallion.
Planting botanicals,
All I smell is pine, and I feel the
crisp air of November.
It feels great deriving through the
countryside,
A new chapter.

I claim this exuberance behind this
new masterpiece, Shed old parts of
me like a withering bush.
Uncovering seeds planted but
couldn't grow because the ground
was frozen,
This breathtaking view is what I've
chosen.
I chose peace .

PASSION PLAYS

Let me show you all the ways
with acts of service,
Treating your body as if it
were a sermon,
Touching you in ways that you've
never experienced,
All I need is for you to lock the door
and close the curtains.

Lay back while I perform,
Intoxicated and high off at
this moment.
I want you to crave me until this
cove is what you yearn.
You're not loud enough, I want
to hear you over the music -
expressive like an art form,
Illustrating the room with vibrant
colors that stains the sheets.
So close that we can hear our
heartbeats,
Hiking on the mountain until we
reach my blue lagoon.

Intimate, yet tropical as I swim
around your coral reef,
Surfacing only to catch some air.
Paddling in the canoe, drifting,
Drifting & studying the waters,
Indulging in one another - we don't
care if we sink,
For we have us.

Spreading my legs as you captivate
further into me
Creamy froth pouring over your
coffee.
You love to clean up the mess with
the tip of your tongue.
Speaking to me in different ways
to help guide my love to spray like a
sprinkler on a hot summer day,
Regulating to the size deep into my
honey pot.
Stroke by stroke - gyrating as my
pot grows hot,
Looking you in the eyes, telling you
to give me that shit.

Eyes closing as I brace myself.
More sensations as I grow tighter to
your now swollen erection,
Speeding up the pace until you
spew out your love juices on my
midsection,

Kissing me slowly & lovingly,
Connection deepening - **immersed
in this moment -
this treasured opportunity.**

SKIN DEEP

Beautiful on the outside With
a beautiful soul.
Never allowing anyone to
get too close,
Due to the hurt and pain that she's
gone through.

She disguises her pain with a smile
on her face,
She camouflages her insecurities with an
extra pep in her step.
She is broken from her childhood
trauma,
Thugs her financial difficulties
because she wants to maintain her
independence,
She believes that not a soul is there
for her,
Which is why she suppresses her
head drama.

She is at war but only with herself,
She wants to seek help,

But feels like help only comes if
there is something in return.
Yet, she yearns for someone like
her.
She knows that she's different, so
she maintains her distance.

Grinds like no other,
Still, I want to be able to go home to
rest.
Take a week off to let her hair
down.
She is hideous on the inside due to
her scars,
But hides her darkness while
staying busy.

She knows that her darkness is an
abomination to the world,
So she stays a good girl.

She breathes rapid fire but
extinguishes the flame when
other's presence,
She comprehends that she has to
mellow down sometimes to be
accepted.

Eager to be treated like an equal,
Yet, she knows that she'll never fit
in.
She was meant to stand out, Be

herself,
She is a wild child.

She's a beauty to the world, She
speaks with grace & elegance,
She knows that she is highly
intelligent. She's sacred, so she
treats herself as such, She only
gives a little bit at a time,
She refuses to give herself too
much.

She won't settle for less, She
deserves the best.
She is magical with her words,
But conflicted when it applies to
herself.
She understands the areas where
she needs to heal.
So she works on healing.

She is me, She is you, She is us.

SILHOUETTE

Qualities that I possess,
Makes you want to undress
The mysterious silhouette
of what lies behind the shadows
exposed on the walls.

As the dark slim figure moves
slowly to the beat of the music,
Just a tune that only I am able to
hear.
Looking around to see if anyone else
hears or notices,
But the world passes us by slowly

Who is this person that seems so
good,
But their energy feels so strong?
Hair flowing down the middle of
her spine,
Squinting my eyes, trying to get a
better vision.

Drawing me closer and intriguing my
curiosity,

Her fingers beckon for me to come
closer.

Her body moving in waves as I
ignore my better judgment and
inch closer,

She teleports and grabs my
shoulder, But I'm frozen in a trance.

Seducing me softly with words I
can't understand or hear,
I begin to fantasize on what I would
love to do to her right here.

Circling around,
She undrapes me,
Her nudeness amazes me, Lassoing
me to touch her,
My excitement confuses me of the
places that begin to stir.
I have been beguiled -
No, bamboozled & it's all a blur,

But I love the way she makes me feel.

So dark,
But yet so good at what she does,
Unrestrained, unmatched, & wild.
I smile & take her hand with a smile.

Our silhouettes dance on the wall,
Our sounds become tunes that we
don't care who hears,
As the world passes by.

Eastyn Star

Eastyn Star is the author of Prisoner in My Thoughts, Mirror, and Hello, Sunlight. She is an African-American poet who was born in Los Angeles, California but was raised in Lancaster, California. Her love of poetry grew when she was in the 9th grade. In her Literature class, she was assigned to write her first poem, "You'll Never See Me Fall Apart." After writing her first 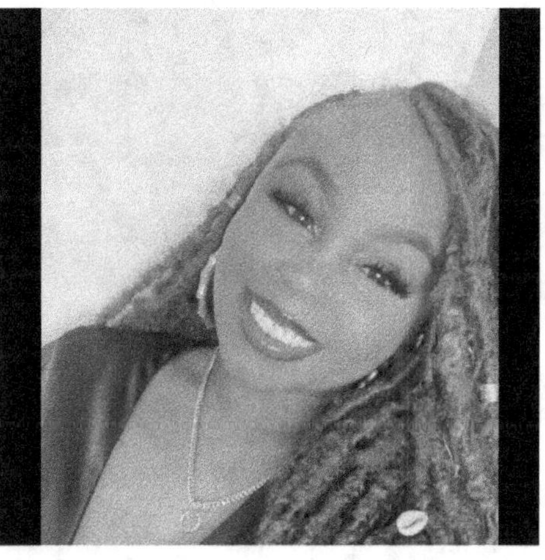 poem, she used poetry throughout the years as an expression, and believes that if she can touch one, she can touch the world through her poetry. Eastyn has written over 350 poems, and continues to find inspiration through spoken word, and writing. Eastyn now lives in California with her three children. When she's not writing, you can find her spending time with her children and family, working with her team, or curled up with a good book and a glass of red wine. Find her on Facebook @Eastyn Star, or on Instagram @eastynstar.

Prisoner In My Thoughts

"Calling for help repetitively, but no one hears me. Screaming at the top of my lungs until my voice grows hoarse, a voice whispers in my head, "Give up, you have run your course," responding back I say, "Not in this lifetime." "I am a strong woman, a survivor, and I will make it out of here alive."Prisoner in My Thoughts is a collection of quotes and poetry. Diving into themes of life, love, and unforgettable experiences. Above all else, being inspired through the reader's own recollection of love and heartbreak. Peeking into the writer's mind showing a visual of how deep and dark suppressed emotions can be. Silently crying for help and liberation from the very shadow that's trying to take hold of the mental state of mind and destroy it. Prisoner in My Thoughts takes you on a journey to let readers know that they're not alone.

Mirror

"Ran around and started finding me until I found her.

Now that I found her, I found her curled up in a corner, & covered with dirt.

Bruised & bloody. I tried to approach her, but she flinched.

I tried to touch her, & she put her arms out to shield herself as if I was dangerous.

Speaking softly, she listened. Inexplicably sizing me from head to toe.

Through watery eyes, she said "It's time."

Mirror is the depths and the ending of Prisoner in My Thoughts with more quotes, love, and heartbreaking with self-discovery poems. Depending on her intuition and listening to her body as the writer submerges into the pool of depression with barely holding on, she decided that "ENOUGH IS ENOUGH." This book is a full visual of the writer begging and pleading for the road to end the pain and suffering with hopes of redemption. Mirror is a reflection of the writer's thoughts as she moves forward with self-healing. Further giving the readers a glimpse of how it feels to face their own personal deepest yet darkest moments in the mirror.

9 798861 278874